35 Diabetic Meal Recipes:

The Most Delicious Way to Stay Healthy

By

Joseph Correa

Certified Sports Nutritionist

COPYRIGHT

© 2016 Finibi Inc

All rights reserved

Reproduction or translation of any part of this work beyond that permitted by section 107 or 108 of the 1976 United States Copyright Act without the permission of the copyright owner is unlawful.

This publication is designed to provide accurate and authoritative information in regard to the subject matter covered. It is sold with the understanding that neither the author nor the publisher is engaged in rendering medical advice. If medical advice or assistance is needed, consult with a doctor. This book is considered a guide and should not be used in any way detrimental to your health. Consult with a physician before starting this nutritional plan to make sure it's right for you.

ACKNOWLEDGEMENTS

The realization and success of this book could not have been possible without the motivation and support of my entire family.

35 Diabetic Meal Recipes:

The Most Delicious Way to Stay Healthy

By

Joseph Correa

Certified Sports Nutritionist

CONTENTS

Copyright

Acknowledgements

About The Author

Introduction

What is Diabetes?

How Do You Manage Diabetes?

What Should You Eat?

Calendar

35 Diabetic Meal Recipes: The Most Delicious Way to Stay Healthy

Other Great Titles by This Author

ABOUT THE AUTHOR

As a certified sports nutritionist, I honestly believe in the positive effects that proper nutrition can have over the body and mind. My knowledge and experience has helped me live healthier throughout the years and which I have shared with family and friends. The more you know about eating and drinking healthier, the sooner you will want to change your life and eating habits.

Nutrition is a key part in the process of being healthy and living longer so get started today.

INTRODUCTION

35 Diabetic Meal Recipes: The Most Delicious Way to Stay Healthy will help you control your high blood glucose levels naturally and effectively. These are not to replace meals but should complement your normal day to day meals.

Being too busy to eat right can sometimes become a problem and that's why this book will save you time and help nourish your body to achieve the goals you want.

This book will help you to:

-Control high blood glucose levels.

-Improve metabolism.

-Have more energy.

-Improve your digestive system.

Joseph Correa is a certified sports nutritionist and a professional athlete.

WHAT IS DIABETES?

Diabetes is a metabolic disease in which a person has high blood glucose levels also known as high blood sugar. Glucose is one of the most important substances that cells use in order to produce energy, but in order for glucose to enter these cells, 2 conditions are required: the cells must have 'doors' called receptors, and a hormone called insulin must be available to 'unlock' these receptors. A lack in receptors or insulin will lead to glucose accumulating in the blood stream with negative effect on your health.

Depending of which part of this mechanism is faulty, there are 2 types of diabetes. Type 1 diabetes occurs when the insulin producing cells in the pancreas are destroyed which leads to high blood sugar. Type 2 diabetes occurs when there is enough insulin but there are not enough receptors on the cells to allow glucose to enter, thus causing an increase in blood sugar.

HOW DO YOU MANAGE DIABETES?

An important aspect in managing this disease is a healthy and balanced diet.

Blood sugar can be controlled successfully by paying attention to what and how much you eat and by maintaining an optimal weight.

While people with type 1 diabetes need insulin, in early diagnosed cases of type 2 diabetes, diet and lifestyle changes can control blood glucose level so well that medication is not needed.

So let's see what dietary recommendations you should follow:

1. Eat a variety of food. All food groups should be included in a healthy diet plan.
2. Eat the amount of food your body needs. This addresses both under and over eating, with focus on the latter, since weight gain is all the more serious for diabetics.
3. Eat a lot of vegetables, grains and fruit. Plants are rich in minerals and vitamins and are cholesterol free.
4. Eat a diet low in saturated fat and cholesterol.

5. Consume foods and drinks such as candy, desserts, sodas and alcohol in moderation. (Or better yet, abstain completely if you can).

WHAT SHOULD YOU EAT?

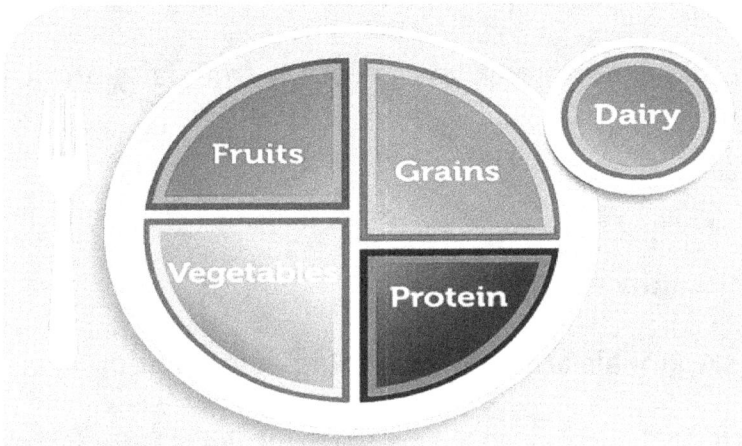

This plate is a guideline for healthy eating and it will help you choose the best foods for a balanced diet.

Vegetables: Eat a variety of vegetables to get all the nutrients that your body requires. Focus on dry beans and peas, dark green and orange vegetables.

Grain: Eat mostly whole grains, since they are less processed and more nutritious. Opt for brown rice, whole wheat, oats, barley and cereal.

Fruit: Eat a variety of fruit, and make sure to go easy on the fruit juices. They are much higher in carbs and lower in fiber.

Protein: The best protein sources are lean meat, poultry, fish, dry beans, eggs, nuts and seeds.

Dairy: Make sure to pick low-fat or fat-free dairy products to lower your fat intake.

Tips for healthy eating:

Do not skip meals and eat something every 4 hours.

Look out for portion size and carb intake. Choose foods that are lower in saturated fat, cholesterol and sodium.

Cook your meals at home and control what you put inside your body.

Try the following recipes and see how delicious healthy eating can become.

CALENDAR

Week 1

Day 1:

Egg and Vegetable Muffins

Snack: Apple and Peanut Butter

Chicken Soup

Snack: Cup of Popcorn

Roasted Cauliflower

Day 2:

Berry Almond Oatmeal

Snack: Veggie Dip

Roast Turkey and Vegetables

Snack: Tomatoes with Cottage Cheese

Cucumber and Cranberry Salad

Day 3:

Peach Smoothie

Snack: Trail Mix

Chicken Drumsticks and Tomatoes

Snack: Ham and Pineapple

Quinoa Pilaf

Day 4:

Quick Omelette

Snack: Smoothie

Poached Salmon with Asparagus

Snack: Pear and Cheese

Roasted Tomatoes

Day 5:

Blueberry Pancakes

Snack: Greek Yogurt with Strawberries

Clam Chowder

Snack: Carrots with Ranch Dressing

Tofu Dinner

Day 6:

Fruit with Yogurt Topping

Snack: Rye Crisps

Mexican Chicken Salad

Snack: Cucumber and Ranch Dressing

Vegetable Lasagna

Day 7:

Smoked Salmon Wraps

Snack: Fresh Fruit Parfait

Ginger Beef Stir-Fry

Snack: Roasted Soy Beans

Eggplant and Arugula Salad

Week 2

Day 1:

Frittata

Snack: Tomatoes with Cottage Cheese

Basil and Tomato Chicken

Snack: Veggie Dip

Falafel Burger

Day 2:

Vegetable Sandwiches

Snack: Cu of Popcorn

Curried Pork

Snack: Apple and Peanut Butter

Chickpea Soup

Day 3:

Breakfast Risotto with Eggs

Snack: Pear and Cheese

Salmon and Vegetable Bake

Snack: Smoothie

Pea and Artichoke Purée

Day 4:

Tofu Scramble

Snack: Trail Mix

Beef Salad

Snack: Ham and Pineapple

Avocado and Grapefruit Salad

Day 5:

Berry Almond Oatmeal

Snack: Rye Crisps

Garlic Shrimp on Spinach

Snack: Cucumber and Ranch Dressing

Grilled Vegetable Salad

Day 6:

Quick Omelette

Snack: Greek Yogurt with Strawberries

Chicken Soup

Carrots with Ranch Dressing

Quinoa Pilaf

Day 7:

Blueberry Pancakes

Snack: Roasted Soy Beans

Ginger Beef Stir-Fry

Snack: Fresh Fruit Parfait

Cucumber and Cranberry Salad

Week 3

Day 1:

Peach Smoothie

Snack: Apple and Peanut Butter

Mexican Chicken Salad

Snack: Veggie Dip

Falafel Burger

Day 2:

Egg and Vegetable Muffins

Snack: Cup of Popcorn

Poached Salmon with Asparagus

Snack: Tomatoes with Cottage Cheese

Roasted Cauliflower

Day 3:

Fruit with Yogurt Topping

Snack: Trail Mix

Garlic Shrimp on Spinach

Snack: Smoothie

Egg and Arugula Salad

Day 4:

Frittata

Snack: Ham and Pineapple

Curried Pork

Snack: Carrots with Ranch Dressing

Pea and Artichoke Purée

Day 5:

Tofu Scramble

Snack: Pear and Cheese

Salmon and Vegetable Bake

Snack: Smoothie

Roasted Tomatoes

Day 6:

Breakfast Risotto with Eggs

Snack: Greek Yogurt with Strawberries

Beef Salad

Snack: Cucumber and Ranch Dressing

Vegetable Lasagna

Day 7:

Vegetable Sandwiches

Snack: Rye Crisps

Clam Chowder

Snack: Roasted Soy Beans

Avocado and Grapefruit Salad

Week 4

Day 1:

Smoked Salmon Wraps

Snack: Fresh Fruit Parfait

Basil and Tomato Chicken

Snack: Veggie Dip

Grilled Vegetable Salad

Day 2:

Blueberry Pancakes

Snack: Cup of Popcorn

Roast Turkey and Vegetables

Snack: Apple and Peanut Butter

Tofu Dinner

Day 3:

Berry Almond Oatmeal

Snack: Tomatoes with Cottage Cheese

Chicken Drumsticks and Tomatoes

Snack: Ham and Pineapple

Chickpea Soup

Day 4:

Quick Omelette

Snack: Trail Mix

Ginger Beef Stir-Fry

Snack: Smoothie

Cucumber and Cranberry Salad

Day 5:

Fruit with Yogurt Topping

Snack: Rye Crisps

Curried Pork

Snack: Carrots with Ranch Dressing

Quinoa Pilaf

Day 6:

Egg and Vegetable Muffins

Snack: Greek Yogurt Strawberries

Poached Salmon with Asparagus

Snack: Roasted Soy Beans

Roasted Cauliflower

Day 7:

Tofu Scramble

Snack: Fresh Fruit Parfait

Clam Chowder

Snack: Veggie Dip

Falafel Burger

2 extra days for a full month

Day 1:

Vegetable Sandwiches

Snack: Trail Mix

Mexican Chicken Salad

Snack: Pear and Cheese

Avocado and Grapefruit Salad

Day 2:

Frittata

Snack: Smoothie

Beef Salad

Snack: Cup of Popcorn

Roasted Tomatoes

35 DIABETIC MEAL RECIPES

BREAKFAST

1. Egg and Vegetable Muffins

Cook eggs in muffin tins for an original and portioned nutritious breakfast. The bulgur adds a nice consistency to this egg centered breakfast, while the vegetables bring color and nutrients to the table.

Ingredients (4 servings):

1/3 cup bulgur

¼ cup zucchini, chopped

¼ cup onion, chopped

1 small tomato, chopped

8 eggs, lightly beaten

½ cup reduced-fat feta cheese, crumbled

1 tablespoon olive oil

1 teaspoon fresh oregano

1 teaspoon fresh rosemary

1/8 teaspoon ground black pepper

2/3 cup water

nonstick cooking spray

Prep time: 15 min

Cooking time: 40-45 min

Preparation:

Preheat the oven to 180C fan/ gas 4. Coat 12 muffin cups with nonstick spray and set aside.

In a small pan combine the bulgur and water, bring to a boil, reduce the heat then simmer, covered, until the bulgur is tender. Drain off any liquid.

Heat the oil in a large skillet and cook the zucchini and onion over medium heat for 5 to 10 min, stirring occasionally. Remove from the heat, add the bulgur, tomato, cheese and stir. Spoon the mixture into the muffin cups.

In a large bowl, whisk together eggs, oregano and pepper. Pour over the vegetable mix in the muffin cups.

Bake for 15 to 18 minutes or until a knife inserted in the center of the muffins comes out clean. Let the muffins cool in a pan for 5 min, then carefully remove them and serve warm.

Nutritional value per serving: 256kcal, 15g carbs (3g fiber, 2g sugar), 15g fat (5g saturated), 14g protein, 12% iron, 14% vitamin A, 30% vitamin B2, 11% vitamin B6, 14% vitamin B9, 22% vitamin B12.

2. Peach Smoothie

Start your day with a delicious, creamy smoothie that packs a nice energy punch and is loaded with bone friendly calcium. Experiment with fruit to mix things up.

Ingredients (1 serving):

250g peach fat-free yogurt with no-calorie sweetener

½ cup fat-free milk

1 cup fresh peaches, sliced

½ cup crushed ice

Prep time: 5 min

No cooking

Preparation:

Combine the fruit, milk and yogurt in a blender. Add the ice, blend until almost smooth and serve.

Nutritional value per serving: 227kcal, 30g carbs (1g fiber, 29g sugar), 2g fat (2g saturated), 17g protein, 70% calcium, 14% magnesium, 18% vitamin A, 13% vitamin C,

11% vitamin B1, 42% vitamin B2, 15% vitamin B5, 31% vitamin B12.

3. Vegetable Sandwiches

Try a refreshing breakfast with zucchini and summer squash that add zest to your morning meal. These well-seasoned veggies topped with grilled mozzarella and wheat bread are crunchy and delicious.

Ingredients (4 servings):

½ medium zucchini, sliced lengthwise

½ medium summer squash, sliced lengthwise

1 small red onion, sliced

1 medium tomato, halved

4 medium slices whole wheat bread

½ cup skim mozzarella cheese, shredded

a pinch of salt

a pinch of ground black pepper

¼ cup basil leaves

nonstick cooking spray

Prep time: 10 min

Cooking time: 15 min

Preparation:

Lightly coat the summer squash, zucchini, tomato and onion with cooking spray then sprinkle with salt and pepper.

Preheat an electric grill. Grill the zucchini, squash and onion until tender, turning them once. Then add the tomatoes and grill until heated through and lightly charred. Grill the bread slices for 1 min, turning once then top with cheese and wait 1 min.

Cut up the vegetables as desired then top the bread slices with the vegetables and basil leaves and serve.

Nutritional value per serving: 201kcal, 28g carbs (4g fiber, 8g sugar), 5g fat (2g saturated), 8g protein, 10% calcium, 11% iron, 14% magnesium, 23% vitamin C, 12% vitamin K, 13% vitamin B1, 13% vitamin B2, 12% vitamin B3, 13% vitamin B6, 14% vitamin B9.

4. Blueberry Pancakes

Boost your energy levels with a serving of delicious blueberry pancakes. Add a spoon of low-fat yogurt and sprinkle some cinnamon as an alternative to the high-carb syrup.

Ingredients (4 servings-8 pancakes):

½ cup buckwheat flour

½ cup whole wheat flour

1 egg

½ teaspoon baking powder

¼ teaspoon baking soda

1¼ cup buttermilk

¾ cup fresh blueberries

¼ teaspoon vanilla

liquid stevia extract

¼ teaspoon salt

1 tablespoon cooking oil

Prep time: 10 min

Cooking time: 20 min

Preparation:

In a bowl, stir together the flour, stevia extract (to taste), baking powder, baking soda and salt. Make a well in the center of the mixture and set aside.

Beat the egg slightly in a small bowl then stir in the buttermilk, oil and vanilla.

Add the buttermilk mixture to the flour mixture, stir until it is combined but slightly lumpy and throw in the blueberries.

Heat a lightly greased heavy skillet over medium heat and pour ¼ cup of batter for each pancake. Spread the batter into a circle that is about 8 cm in diameter.

Cook over medium heat until the pancakes are brow, turning to cook the other side when the pancake surface is bubbly and the edges are slightly dry. Serve while still hot.

Nutritional value per serving (2 pancakes): 198kcal, 30g carbs (4g fiber, 6g sugar), 6g fat, 8g protein, 12% calcium, 17% magnesium, 16% vitamin B2.

5. Smoked Salmon Wraps

Start your day with smoked salmon and make sure you get some of those healthy omega-3 fatty acids. The whole wheat is a great alternative to the 'breakfast bagel' as it is lower in carbs and adds some fiber to the mix.

Ingredients (2 servings):

85g smoked salmon, cut into strips

¼ cup light cream cheese spread

2*15 cm whole wheat flour tortillas

½ small zucchini, peeled into ribbons

1 teaspoon fresh chives

½ teaspoon lemon peel, finely shredded

1 teaspoon lemon juice

Prep time: 10 min

No cooking

Preparation:

In a small bowl, stir together the cream cheese, lemon juice and peel and chives until smooth. Spread evenly over the 2 tortillas leaving a small border around the edges.

Divide the salmon among the tortillas; place the zucchini ribbons on top of the salmon.

Roll up the tortillas and serve them cut in half.

Nutritional value per serving: 255kcal, 29g carbs (3g fiber, 4g sugar), 8g fat (3g saturated), 14g protein, 10% vitamin B3, 27% vitamin B12.

6. Quick Omelette

A 5 minute omelette with a vitamin K kick, this breakfast meal is high in protein and low in carbs and is bound to fill you up till lunch. Serve with a few cherry tomatoes for some extra vitamin C.

Ingredients (2 servings):

4 eggs

1 cup fresh baby spinach leaves

¼ cup reduced-fat cheddar cheese, shredded

1 tablespoon flat-leaf parsley

a pinch of salt

a pinch of cayenne pepper

nonstick cooking spray

Prep time: 5 min

Cooking time: 5 min

Preparation:

Coat a nonstick skillet with cooking spray and heat over medium heat.

In a large bowl, combine the eggs, chives, pepper and salt and whisk until frothy.

Pour into the skillet and start stirring the eggs gently with a plastic spatula until the mixture resembles small pieces of cooked egg surrounded by liquid egg. Stop stirring and cook for 30s to 1 min until the eggs are set but shiny.

Sprinkle with cheese, top with the spinach, fold the omelette and serve.

Nutritional value per serving: 185kcal, 2g carbs, 11g fat (3g saturated), 17g protein, 13% calcium, 12% iron, 38% vitamin A, 90% vitamin K, 31% vitamin B2, 14% vitamin B5, 20% vitamin B12.

7. Berry Almond Oatmeal

Low in fat and high in soluble fiber, oatmeal is a great breakfast option since it helps with appetite control and lowers glucose levels. Add some raspberries for a smoother taste and serve with a glass of skim milk to get half a day's worth of calcium.

Ingredients (1 serving):

½ cup cooked oatmeal

6 almonds, chopped

1 cup raspberries

1 cup skim milk

Prep time: 5 min

No cooking:

Preparation:

Stir in the raspberries and almonds into a bowl of hot cooked oatmeal. Serve with a glass of milk.

Nutritional value per serving: 256kcal, 44g carbs (10g fiber, 17g sugar), 5g fat, 13g protein, 56% calcium, 13% iron, 32% magnesium, 24% vitamin A, 58% vitamin C, 20% vitamin E, 12% vitamin K, 15% vitamin B1, 27% vitamin B2, 11% vitamin B9, 16% vitamin B12.

8. Tofu Scramble

Replace cheese with vegetarian friendly tofu and enjoy the added protein and the healthy fats that come with that. Spice this veggie delight with fresh chili pepper and start your day at full throttle.

Ingredients (1 serving):

225g extra-firm water-packed tofu

½ cup plum tomatoes, chopped

1 clove of garlic, minced

¼ cup onion, chopped

1 fresh chili pepper, deseeded and chopped

1 teaspoon olive oil

½ teaspoon chili powder

1/8 teaspoon salt

1 teaspoon lime juice

¼ teaspoon ground cumin

¼ teaspoon dried oregano

Fresh cilantro sprigs (optional)

Prep time: 10 min

Cooking time: 10 min

Preparation:

Drain the tofu, cut it in half and pat each half with paper towels until well dried. Crumble the tofu into a bowl and set aside.

Heat the olive oil over medium heat in a large nonstick skillet. Add the pepper, onion, garlic and cook for 4 min. Put in the seasoning and cook for 30s then add the crumbled tofu into the mixture. Reduce the heat, cook for 5 min stirring occasionally. Serve with lime juice, tomatoes and fresh cilantro.

Nutritional value per serving: 229kcal, 7g carbs (1g fiber, 4 g sugar), 13g fat (1g saturated), 16g protein, 49% calcium, 25% iron, 27% magnesium, 12% vitamin A, 21% vitamin C, 18% vitamin K, 11% vitamin B1, 13% vitamin B6, 13% vitamin B9.

9. Fruit with Yogurt Topping

Make your own fruit yogurt with fresh ingredients and natural sources of carbs. The pineapple and vanilla make for a delicious combination, but any fruit that you like will do the trick.

Ingredients (2 servings):

1 cup plain low-fat yogurt

200g pineapple, crushed

1 cup fresh strawberries, halved

1 teaspoon vanilla

Prep time: 5 min

No cooking

Preparation:

Stir together the yogurt, crushed pineapple and vanilla. Cover and chill for 1 hour (or overnight).

Divide half the yogurt between 2 bowls, add the strawberries. Topple with the rest of the yogurt and serve.

Nutritional value per serving: 160kcal, 27g carbs (4g fiber, 22g sugar), 2g fat (1g saturated), 8g protein, 24% calcium, 10% magnesium, 156% vitamin C, 18% vitamin B2, 10% vitamin B5, 11% vitamin B6, 18% vitamin B9, 11% vitamin B12.

10. Breakfast Risotto with Eggs

Look outside the box and try risotto for breakfast. Made breakfast friendly by replacing rice with steel-cut oats, this dish gets its savory touches from the sautéed veggie and the Brie cheese.

Ingredients (4 servings):

4 eggs

½ cup steel-cut oats

1½ cups water

½ cup red pepper chopped

½ cup fresh button mushrooms, sliced

40g reduced-fat brie cheese, rind removed

1 cup fresh spinach, chopped

1 spring onion, sliced

a pinch of salt

1/8 cup fresh basil, snipped

Ground black pepper

Nonstick cooking spray

Prep time: 5 min

Cooking time: 15 min

Preparation:

Heat a nonstick pan after coating it with nonstick spray. Add the bell pepper and mushrooms and cook for 5 min, stirring occasionally. Add the spring onions, cook for 3 min then remove the vegetables and set aside.

Add the oats in the pan used to cook the vegetables, stir the 1 ½ cup of hot water into the oats and cook until the liquid is absorbed. When the oats are tender remove the mixture form the heat, add the cheese and stir until it has melted and the mixture is well combined. Add the spinach and the vegetable mix.

Coat a nonstick skillet with nonstick spray and heat over medium heat. Break the eggs into the skillet, making sure they remain separate. Reduce the heat to low, cook the eggs until the whites are completely done and the yolks start to thicken. Flick the eggs and cook for 30s if you prefer them over easy or 1 min for over hard.

Spoon the oat mixture into 4 bowls, top each serving with the fried egg, sprinkle with pepper and basil then serve.

Nutritional value per serving: 197kcal, 15g carbs (2g fiber, 1g sugar), 8g fat (2g saturated), 12g protein, 12% iron, 12% magnesium, 10% vitamin A, 30% vitamin C, 57% vitamin K, 14% vitamin B1, 19% vitamin B2, 11% vitamin B5, 14% vitamin B9, 11% vitamin B12.

11. Frittata

This vegetable-loaded frittata made with egg whites, is low in cholesterol and high in protein which makes for a very nutritious breakfast. If you like, you can replace the feta cheese with goat or Parmesan cheese.

Ingredients (2 servings):

3 eggs

6 egg whites

2 cups small broccoli florets

1 cup cherry tomatoes, quartered

¼ cup feta cheese

2 tablespoons shallots, finely chopped

¼ teaspoon salt and ground black pepper

nonstick cooking spray

Prep time: 10 min

Cooking time: 15-20 min

Preparation:

In a medium bowl, whisk together the egg whites, eggs, salt and pepper, then stir in the cheese and set aside.

Heat the oil over medium heat in a nonstick pan and cook the broccoli and shallots for 8 to10 min, stirring occasionally. Pour the egg mixture and cook over medium-low heat until the mixture sets. Using a spatula, lift the edges so that the uncooked portion flows underneath. When the eggs are cooked arrange the tomatoes on top of the egg mixture.

Let it stand for 5 min, cut into 4 wedges and serve.

Nutritional value per serving: 270kcal, 10g carbs (3g fiber, 4g sugar), 12g fat (5g saturated), 26g protein, 19% calcium, 13% iron, 14% magnesium, 32% vitamin A, 151% vitamin C, 123% vitamin K, 11% vitamin B1, 68% vitamin B2, 20% vitamin B5, 21% vitamin B6, 28% vitamin B9, 23% vitamin B12.

LUNCH

12. Roast Turkey and Vegetables

This herb-infused roast and vegetable combo is a great pick for lunch and it will delight your taste buds. Packed with protein and vitamin A, this dish makes for a filling and nutritious meal.

Ingredients (2 servings):

300g turkey breast, skin removed

200g small red potatoes, quartered

1 cup baby carrots, halved lengthwise

1 cup red pearl onion, halved

2 cloves garlic, minced

1 tablespoon fresh parsley

½ teaspoon fresh rosemary

½ teaspoon fresh thyme

1 teaspoon olive oil

¼ teaspoon salt

¼ teaspoon ground black pepper

Nonstick cooking spray

Prep time: 10 min

Cooking time: 2 h

Preparation:

Preheat the oven to 200C fan/ gas 6. Combine the rosemary, parsley, garlic, thyme, salt and pepper in a small bowl. Set aside 1 teaspoon of the herb mixture.

Place the turkey breast on a roasting rack in a roasting pan. Lightly coat with the nonstick cooking spray, sprinkle the remaining herb mixture evenly over the turkey and rub it in with your fingers then roast, uncovered, for 20 min.

Combine the carrots, pearl onions and potatoes in a large bowl and add the reserved teaspoon of herb mixture, the olive oil then toss until the vegetables are coated. Arrange the vegetables around the turkey in the roasting pan.

Reduce the oven temperature to 180C fan/ gas 4 and roast for about 1 ½ hours or until the juices run clear and the turkey is no longer pink. Stir the vegetables once.

Transfer the turkey to a cutting board, then cover with foil and let it stand for 10 min. Carve the turkey, divide the pieces and the vegetables between 2 plates and serve.

Nutritional value per serving: 315kcal, 38g carbs (5g fiber, 14g sugar), 5g fat, 29g protein, 21% iron, 17% magnesium, 235% vitamin A, 60% vitamin C, 14% vitamin K, 23% vitamin B1, 34% vitamin B2, 10% vitamin B5, 33% vitamin B6, 15% vitamin B9.

13. Garlic Shrimp on Spinach

Pair fresh spinach and garlicky shrimp to make a low-calorie, low-carb, highly nutritious meal. The Parmesan cheese sprinkling is a great way to accentuate the flavor of this dish.

Ingredients (2 servings):

250g fresh or frozen medium shrimp in shells

4 cups fresh spinach

2 cloves garlic, minced

½ teaspoon lemon peel, finely shredded

1 tablespoon olive oil

1 tablespoon Parmesan cheese, shredded

a pinch of ground black pepper

Prep time: 5 min

Cooking time: 10 min

Preparation:

Thaw the shrimp if frozen. Peel and devein the shrimp. In a small bowl, toss together the shrimp, garlic, lemon peel, oil and pepper.

Place a steamer basket in a wok with a tight-fitting lid; add water to just below the basket.

Place the shrimp in a single layer in the steamer basket, cover and steam for 5 to 6 min over medium-high heat. Remove the shrimp and keep warm.

Add the spinach in the steamer basket and steam for 2 min/until wilted.

Divide the spinach between two plates, place the shrimp on top of the spinach, sprinkle with Parmesan cheese and serve.

Nutritional value per serving: 220kcal, 3g carbs (2g fiber), 9g fat (1g saturated), 11g protein, 15% calcium, 26% iron, 24% magnesium, 116% vitamin A, 32% vitamin C, 22% vitamin E, 367% vitamin K, 13% vitamin B3, 12% vitamin B6, 31% vitamin B9, 25% vitamin B12.

14. Beef Salad

Beef is a filling and protein-packed meal option and its pairing with greens makes for a healthy and colorful lunch. A dash of honey adds sweetness and texture to an already nutritious salad.

Ingredients (4 servings):

340g beef flank steak

6 cups mixed salad greens

2 small tomatoes, cut into wedges

½ teaspoon lime peel, finely shredded

1/3 cup lime juice

¼ cup onion, chopped

1 clove garlic, minced

2 tablespoons honey

2 tablespoons olive oil

2 tablespoons powdered fruit pectin

6 tablespoons water

Prep time: 10 min

Cooking time: 30 min

Preparation:

Combine the lime juice, peel, 3 tablespoons of water and olive oil in a crew-top jar then cover and shake well. Pour half of the lime mixture into a bowl, stir in the onion and garlic. Put the remaining juice mixture aside.

Score the beef by making shallow diagonal cuts at 2 cm intervals in a diamond patter, repeat on the other side, then place the beef in a plastic bag and in a shallow dish. Pour the lime juice mixture over the beef, close the bag and marinate in the refrigerator for 24 hours, turning occasionally.

Make the dressing by gradually stirring the water into the fruit pectin. Add the lime juice mixture and honey, cover and chill for 24 hours.

Drain the beef, discard the marinade then place the beef on the unheated rack of a broiler pan. Broil 4 to 6 cm from the heat to desired doneness, turning once.

Arrange the tomatoes and greens on 2 plates, top with thinly sliced pieces of beef, drizzle with the dressing and serve.

Nutritional value per serving: 252kcal, 14g carbs (2g fiber, 10g sugar), 7g fat (2g saturated), 18g protein, 14% iron, 31% vitamin C, 20% vitamin B3, 20% vitamin B6, 25% vitamin B12.

15. Chicken Drumsticks and Tomatoes

This Louisiana inspired recipe brings flavor to a low-carb chicken. The whole grain noodles ensure a healthy serving of quality carbs, while the hot sauce spices up an otherwise simple tasting meal.

Ingredients (2 servings):

2 chicken drumsticks, bones removed

½ cup frozen cut okra

1 cup whole grain noodles, cooked

1*200g can stewed tomatoes (no salt)

½ teaspoon dried thyme, ground

1 teaspoon hot sauce

a pinch of salt

a pinch of black pepper

nonstick cooking spray

Prep time: 5 min

Cooking time: 40 min

Preparation:

Coat a large nonstick skillet with cooking spray and place over medium-high heat. Brown the chicken on all sides for about 6 min, turning occasionally. Add the stewed tomatoes, okra, thyme, 2/3 of the hot sauce, salt and pepper, then bring to a boil. Reduce heat, cover and simmer for 30 min.

Place the chicken on 2 serving plates, stir the remaining hot sauce into the skillet and spoon sauce all over it. Serve with noodles.

Nutritional value per serving: 245kcal, 26g carbs (5g fiber, 5g sugar), 6g fat (2g saturated), 18g protein, 16% iron, 15% magnesium, 21% vitamin C, 23% vitamin K, 14% vitamin B1, 14% vitamin B2, 27% vitamin B3, 14% vitamin B5, 16% vitamin B6, 14% vitamin B9.

16. Clam Chowder

Make a healthier version of the clam chowder by lowering the amount of potatoes and adding some chopped cauliflower. You will still enjoy the richness of the dish, and a few more nutrients without losing any flavor.

Ingredients (2 servings):

1*280g can whole baby clams

1 slice turkey bacon, halved

1½ cups fat-free milk

½ cup carrots, coarsely shredded

½ medium onion, chopped

½ stalk celery, thinly sliced

1 medium potato, cut in 1 cm pieces

1 cup cauliflower florets, cut into 1 cm pieces

a pinch of dry thyme, crushed

a pinch of ground black pepper

1 tablespoon all-purpose flower

water

nonstick cooking spray

Prep time: 10 min

Cooking time: 25 min

Preparation:

Drain the clams, reserving the liquid. Chop half of the clams and set them aside. Add enough water to the reserved clam liquid to measure ¾ cups and set the liquid aside.

Coat a saucepan with cooking spray then heat it over medium heat. Add the bacon, celery and onion, cook for 5 to 8 min stirring occasionally. Remove the bacon from the pan, drain on paper towels and set aside.

Stir the potatoes, cauliflower, pepper, thyme and reserved clam liquid into the onion mixture. Bring to boiling then reduce heat, cover and let it simmer for 10 to 12 min. Remove from heat and cool slightly. Transfer half of the potato mixture to a food processor and blend until smooth. Return the remaining potato mixture in the saucepan.

Whisk together the milk and flour in a medium bowl, add all the potato mixture then cook and stir until boiling. Add the chopped and whole clams and carrots, return to boiling, reduce heat and cook for 1 more minute.

Divide the chowder into 2 bowls and serve with chopped bacon.

Nutritional value per serving: 178kcal, 28g carbs (5g fiber, 4g sugar), 4g fat (1g saturated), 6g protein, 14% magnesium, 103% vitamin A, 82% vitamin C, 22% vitamin K, 11% vitamin B1, 12% vitamin B3, 23% vitamin B6, 16% vitamin B9, 110% vitamin B12.

17. Curried Pork

Be creative and experience an interesting side of pork that owes its fruity flavor to pineapple juice and apple. This protein packed meal has the advantage of being ready in just 15 min.

Ingredients (2 servings):

2*170g boneless pork loin chops

½ cup unsweetened pineapple juice

2 cups Napa cabbage, shredded

½ medium green cooking apple, cut into wedges

1 tablespoon spring onion, sliced

1 teaspoon curry powder

a pinch of salt

a pinch of ground black pepper

Prep time: 5 min

Cooking time: 10 min

Preparation:

Trim the fat from the chops and place them in a pressure cooker. Combine the pineapple juice, salt, pepper and curry powder and pour over the meat.

Lock the lid in place. Bring the cooker up to 7 kg pressure over high heat then reduce the heat enough to maintain high pressure. Cook for 3 min then remove the cooker from the heat and allow the pressure to decrease naturally. Carefully remove the lid and using a slotted spoon transfer the chops to a platter and cover to keep warm.

Bring the liquid in the cooker to boiling, add the apple, reduce the heat and simmer uncovered for 3 minutes, stirring occasionally. Add the cabbage and green onion, cook for 1 to 2 min and using a slotted spoon, transfer the vegetable mixture to the platter with the pork. Spoon the liquid over the chops and apple mixture and serve.

Nutritional value per serving: 300kcal, 17g carbs (2g fiber, 11g sugar), 6g fat (1g saturated), 39g protein, 13% magnesium, 26% vitamin A, 94% vitamin C, 61% vitamin B1, 22% vitamin B2, 60% vitamin B3, 12% vitamin B5, 68% vitamin B6, 14% vitamin B12.

18. Salmon and Vegetable Bake

Get a low-carb, high-protein lunch with little effort. Simply bake salmon fillets between savory vegetables and sweet orange slices and enjoy a highly nutritious meal.

Ingredients (2 servings):

200g fresh or frozen skinless salmon

1 cup carrot, thinly sliced

1 cup mushrooms, sliced

¼ cup spring onions, sliced

2 cloves garlic, halved

1 medium orange, sliced

1 teaspoon orange peel, finely shredded

1 tablespoon olive oil

1 teaspoon fresh oregano

a pinch of salt

a pinch of black pepper

Prep time: 10 min

Cooking time: 30 min

Preparation:

Thaw the salmon, if frozen then rinse it and pat it dry with paper towels and set aside.

Bring some water to boil and cook the carrots for 2 min, drain and set aside.

In a large bowl, combine the carrots, mushrooms, onions, orange peel, oregano, garlic, salt and pepper and toss gently.

Divide the vegetables among the 2 pieces of foil, placing them in the center of each piece. Place the salmon on top of each portion of vegetables, drizzle 1 teaspoon of oil on each piece of salmon and sprinkle with additional salt and pepper. Top with the orange slices then bring together two opposite edges of foil and seal with a double fold. Place the foil packets in a single layer in a baking pan.

Bake at 180C fan/ gas 4 for about 30 min. Open carefully to allow the steam to escape then transfer the packets to 2 plates and serve.

Nutritional value per serving: 190kcal, 15g carbs (4g fiber, 10g sugar), 3g fat (1g saturated), 22g protein, 11% magnesium, 221% vitamin A, 69% vitamin C, 43% vitamin

K, 20% vitamin B1, 16% vitamin B2, 46% vitamin B3, 15% vitamin B5, 19% vitamin B6, 12% vitamin B9, 50% vitamin B12.

19. Mexican Chicken Salad

Enjoy a vitamin- and protein-packed meal that takes only 15 min to make. Add spices to the broiled chicken breasts and a pairing of orange and avocado for a refreshing spin.

Ingredients (2 servings):

2*120g pieces of chicken breast

2 cups romaine lettuce, shredded

½ avocado, sliced

1 orange, sliced

25g Monterey Jack Cheese, shredded

½ teaspoon chili powder

¼ teaspoon dried oregano

¼ teaspoon dried thyme

1 tablespoon orange juice

1 teaspoon olive oil

1 teaspoon wine vinegar

½ teaspoon honey

a pinch of salt

a pinch of ground black pepper

Prep time: 5 min

Cooking time: 10 min

Preparation:

Place the chicken between 2 pieces of plastic wrap each. Pound the chicken with the meat pallet until it is 1 cm thick and remove the plastic wrap.

Preheat the broiler. In a small bowl, stir together the oregano, thyme, chili powder, salt and black pepper. Sprinkle and rub the spice mixture evenly over the chicken pieces.

Place the chicken on the unheated rack of a broiler pan and broil 5 to 7 cm from the heat for 6 to 8 min, turning once halfway through broiling. Remove and slice the chicken.

Whisk together the orange juice, vinegar and honey in a medium bowl. Add lettuce and toss to coat.

Divide the lettuce between 2 plates, top with the sliced chicken, avocado and orange slices, sprinkle with cheese and serve.

Nutritional value per serving: 330kcal, 18g carbs (6g fiber, 11g sugar), 13g fat (3g saturated), 32g protein, 10% iron, 15% magnesium, 86% vitamin A, 87% vitamin C, 74% vitamin K, 14% vitamin B1, 13% vitamin B2, 72% vitamin B3, 19% vitamin B5, 42% vitamin B6, 32% vitamin B9.

20. Ginger Beef Stir-Fry

Add a pop of color to this high-protein beef stir-fry with a hearty serving of vegetables. The brown rice is an excellent option for a healthy dose of quality carbs.

Ingredients (2 servings):

200g boneless beef sirloin steak

1 cup hot cooked brown rice

½ cup reduced-sodium chicken broth

1 clove garlic, minced

1 medium red bell pepper, cut into strips

1 cup broccoli florets

½ medium onion, sliced

1 teaspoon cornstarch

½ teaspoon ground coriander

1 teaspoon sesame oil

Prep time: 10 min

Cooking time: 10 min

Preparation:

Thinly slice the meat across the grain into bite-sized strips then set aside.

Stir together the chicken broth, cornstarch, ginger, coriander and set aside.

Heat the sesame oil over medium-heat in a wok, add the onion and cook for 2 min, add the broccoli and sweet pepper, cook and stir for 1 to 2 min then remove the vegetables from the wok.

Add the beef strips to the wok, cook for 2 to 3 min then push the meat from the center of the wok.

Add the sauce to the center of the wok, cook until thickened and bubbly then return the vegetables to the wok. Make sure to coat all the ingredients with sauce. Cook and stir for 1 to 2 min more and serve immediately with brown rice.

Nutritional value per serving: 368kcal, 31g carbs (4g fiber, 3g sugar), 16g fat (5g saturated), 26g protein, 14% iron, 20% magnesium, 10% vitamin A, 150% vitamin C, 66% vitamin K, 15% vitamin B1, 12% vitamin B2, 40% vitamin B3, 12% vitamin B5, 14% vitamin B9, 18% vitamin B12.

21. Basil and Tomato Chicken

Replenish you vitamin stores with a rich serving of spinach that is a lovely addition to this basil-infused chicken breast. Sprinkle with some Parmesan cheese for an extra hint of flavor.

Ingredients (2 servings):

200g chicken breast tenderloins

1*200g canned tomatoes, diced and drained

4 cups fresh spinach

1 tablespoon Parmesan cheese, shredded

1/8 cup fresh basil

a pinch of salt

a pinch of ground black pepper

nonstick cooking spray

Prep time: 10 min

Cooking time: 8 min

Preparation:

Cut any large tenderloins in half, lengthwise. Coat an unheated skillet with nonstick spray, cook and stir the chicken for about 5 min. Sprinkle with salt and pepper.

Add tomatoes and basil, heat through then remove from heat and add the spinach, tossing until wilted.

Divide among 2 plates, sprinkle with cheese and serve.

Nutritional value per serving: 161kcal, 8g carbs (3g fiber, 4g sugar), 1g fat, 22g protein, 13% calcium, 21% iron, 22% magnesium, 115% vitamin A, 43% vitamin C, 11% vitamin E, 365% vitamin K, 12% vitamin B1, 13% vitamin B2, 60% vitamin B3, 34% vitamin B6, 32% vitamin B9.

22. Poached Salmon with Asparagus   sprinkle parsley

Try poaching some salmon with a fast cooking method that enables food to absorb flavor without fat. The buttery citrus dressing is a great choice for coating fish, while an extra sprinkle of parsley will give the dish a more refreshing taste.

Ingredients (2 servings):

2*100g fresh skinless salmon fillets

220g asparagus spears, woody bases removed

orange juice from 1 orange

lemon juice from ½ lemon

1 teaspoon shredded lemon peel

1 teaspoon melted butter

1 tablespoon fresh parsley

a pinch of salt

a pinch of pepper

½ cup of water

Prep time: 5 min

Cooking time: 10 min

Preparation:

Rinse the fish and pat dry with paper towels. Combine the lemon and orange juices, measure 1/8 cup for the dressing and set aside.

Pour the remaining juice into a skillet, add water and bring to boiling. Add the salmon, reduce the heat to medium and simmer, covered, for 4 min. Lay the asparagus on top of the salmon and simmer for 4 to 8 min or until the fish begins to flake when tested with a fork and the asparagus is crisp.

Combine the rest of the juice, parsley, lemon peel, butter, salt and pepper in a bowl.

Drizzle the dressing mixture over the salmon and asparagus and serve.

Nutritional value per serving: 182kcal, 9g carbs (2g fiber, 5g sugar), 5g fat (2g saturated), 21g protein, 16% iron, 10% magnesium, 19% vitamin A, 52% vitamin K, 23% vitamin B1, 13% vitamin B2, 41% vitamin B3, 11% vitamin B5, 16% vitamin B6, 17% vitamin B9, 50% vitamin B12.

23. Chicken Soup

Add some extra texture and flavor to this healthy chicken soup with serving of barley. High in protein and low in carbs, this meal is a perfect choice for balancing your daily carb intake.

Ingredients (3 servings):

400g boneless chicken breast, cut into bite-size pieces

200g potatoes, cubed

½ cup mushrooms, chopped

½ cup carrots, chopped

¼ cup onion, chopped

¼ cup chopped green sweet pepper

2 cloves garlic

1 teaspoon fresh basil

1 teaspoon fresh parsley

½ teaspoon poultry seasoning

¼ cup quick-cooking barley

1 tablespoon olive oil

1 tablespoon chicken bouillon granules

a pinch of ground black pepper

a pinch of salt

Prep time: 10 min

Cooking time: 25 min

Preparation:

Toss the chicken pieces with the poultry seasoning and set aside.

Heat half the olive oil in a Dutch oven, add the carrots, mushroom, onion, sweet pepper, garlic, black pepper and salt then cook for 10 min, stirring occasionally. Remove the vegetables from the oven and set aside.

Add the remaining olive oil to the Dutch oven, heat over medium heat, add the chicken and cook for about 5 min. Return the vegetables to the oven, stir in the watered chicken bouillon granules and bring to a boil. Stir in the potatoes and barley, return to boiling and reduce the heat. Cover and simmer until the potatoes are tender (about 15 min). Stir in the fresh parsley and basil, scoop into 4 bowls and serve.

Nutritional value per serving: 255kcal, 16g carbs (2g fiber, 2g sugar), 6g fat, 32g protein, 15% magnesium, 80% vitamin A, 29% vitamin C, 81% vitamin B3, 22% vitamin B5, 50% vitamin B6.

DINNER

24. Roasted Cauliflower

Easy to make, with few ingredients, this recipe is both filling and low in carbs. Give cauliflower a bit of zing by adding red onion and coriander to make a vitamin C-packed dish.

Ingredients (2 servings):

1 medium cauliflower (around 575g), cut into florets

2 medium red onions, sliced into thick wedges

1 teaspoon ground coriander

2 tablespoons olive oil

a handful fresh coriander, to serve

a pinch of salt

a pinch of pepper

Prep time: 5 min

Cooking time: 25 min

Preparation:

Heat the oven to 200C fan/ gas 7. Toss the cauliflower, red onion, coriander and olive oil together with some salt and pepper in a roasting tin. Roast for 25 min, tossing occasionally until the vegetables start to brown.

Serve with fresh coriander.

Nutritional value per serving: 235kcal, 25g carbs (9g fiber, 12g sugar), 14g fat (2g saturated), 6g protein, 236% vitamin C, 63% vitamin K, 14% vitamin B1, 12% vitamin B2, 19% vitamin B5, 38% vitamin B6, 46% vitamin B9.

25. Vegetable Lasagna

Try a tasty lasagna that cuts down on the calories by replacing meat with vegetables, making it a perfect option for dinner. You can cut down on calories even more by using light pasta sauce.

Ingredients (8 servings):

6 dried whole wheat lasagna noodles

1 medium tomato, chopped

2 medium zucchinis, halved lengthwise and sliced

2 cups fresh mushrooms, sliced

1 small onion, chopped

1 cup light ricotta cheese

3 tablespoons Parmesan cheese, finely shredded

1 cup part-skim mozzarella cheese, shredded

2 cups pasta sauce

¼ cup fresh parsley, snipped

¼ teaspoon black pepper

1 tablespoon olive oil

Prep time: 15 min

Cooking time: 40 min

Preparation:

Cook the noodles according to the instructions on the pack, then drain and rinse with cold water.

Heat the oil in a nonstick skillet, add the mushrooms, squash and onion and cook over medium-heat for about 5 min. Remove from heat and set aside. In a small bowl, combine the Parmesan and ricotta cheese, parsley and pepper.

Assemble the lasagna by placing 3 lasagna noodles on the bottom of a baking dish and trimming them to fit if necessary. Spoon half of the cheese mixture over the noodles, top with half of the vegetable mixture, half of the sauce and half of the mozzarella cheese. Layer with the remaining noodles, the rest of the cheese, vegetable mixture and sauce.

Heat the oven to 190C fan/ gas 5. Bake for 30 min then remove the baking dish from the oven, sprinkle with the tomato and remaining mozzarella cheese then bake for another 5 min.

Let the lasagna stand for 10 min then serve.

Nutritional value per serving: 251kcal, 31g carbs (3g fiber, 9g sugar), 9g fat (4g saturated), 14g protein, 23% calcium, 15% magnesium, 17% vitamin A, 21% vitamin C, 17% vitamin K, 12% vitamin B1, 15% vitamin B2, 23% vitamin B3, 16% vitamin B6, 11% vitamin B9.

26. Eggplant and Arugula Salad

Spruce up an eggplant with a side of arugula and raisins that make a very healthy salad that is easy on the stomach. Add a pop of color by adding some dried cranberries to the mix

Ingredients (2 servings):

1 medium eggplant, cut into small chunks

25g arugula

2 miniature box of raisins (about 14g per box)

1 tablespoon balsamic vinegar

1 ½ tablespoon olive oil

a pinch of salt

a pinch of pepper

Prep time: 10 min

Cooking time: 30 min

Preparation:

Heat the oven to 200C fan/ gas 6. Toss the eggplant with 2/3 of the olive oil and seasoning in a roasting tin and roast for 30 min.

When cooked, toss with the raising, vinegar and remaining oil. Scatter over the arugula and serve.

Nutritional value per serving: 207kcal, 29g carbs (10g fiber, 14g sugar), 10g fat (1g saturated), 4g protein, 11% magnesium, 16% vitamin C, 11% vitamin E, 39% vitamin K, 10% vitamin B1, 10% vitamin B3, 13% vitamin B6, 13% vitamin B9.

27. Roasted Tomatoes

Get an all-round healthy dose of nutrients with this veggie friendly dinner, that combines savory tomatoes with crunchy bread crumbs and an herb-infused garlicky dressing. Don't forget the Parmesan cheese for a nuttier taste.

Ingredients (2 servings):

4 medium firm under ripe tomatoes, halves crosswise

2 slices whole wheat bread, made into crumbs

4 cloves garlic, minced

4 tablespoons Parmesan cheese, grated

2 tablespoons balsamic vinegar

2 tablespoons olive oil

1 tablespoon dried basil, crushed

1 teaspoon dried oregano, crushed

½ teaspoon dried rosemary, crushed

¼ teaspoon salt

nonstick cooking spray

Prep time: 10 min

Cooking time: 1h 10 min

Preparation:

Coat an unheated slow cooker with cooking spray. Place the tomatoes, cut sides up in the slow cooker. Combine the vinegar, olive oil, garlic, oregano, rosemary, basil and salt in a small bowl then spoon evenly over the tomatoes.

Cover and cook on a high-heat setting for 1 hour.

Heat a medium nonstick skillet over medium-heat, add the breadcrumbs and cook for 2 to 3 min until lightly browned while stirring constantly. Remove from heat and stir in the Parmesan cheese.

Remove the tomatoes form the cooker and place on a serving platter. Drizzle the cooking liquid evenly over the tomatoes and sprinkle with the bread crumb mixture. Let it stand for 10 min then serve.

Nutritional value per serving: 335kcal, 34g carbs (5g fiber, 8g sugar), 18g fat (4g saturated), 10g protein, 16% calcium, 12% iron, 15% magnesium, 40% vitamin A, 52% vitamin C, 18% vitamin E, 39% vitamin K, 15% vitamin B1, 10% vitamin B2, 16% vitamin B3, 15% vitamin B6, 17% vitamin B9.

28. Falafel Burger

Opt for a lower amount of calories with this chickpea based burger that is both healthy and filling. Serve with a side of tomato salsa and green salad and add a hearty dose of vitamin C to your diet.

Ingredients (2 servings):

200g can chickpeas, rinsed and drained

1 garlic clove, chopped

1 small red onion, chopped

½ teaspoon ground cumin

½ teaspoon ground coriander

¼ teaspoon chili powder

1 tablespoon whole wheat flour

a handful of parsley

1 tablespoon olive oil

a pinch of salt

100g tub tomato salsa

2 cups green salad

1 small whole wheat pita bread, cut into 2 pieces

Prep time: 10 min

Cooking time: 6 min

Preparation:

Pat the chickpeas dry with kitchen paper. Tip into a food processor with the garlic, onion, parsley, spices, flour and salt. Blend until almost smooth then shape into 2 patties.

Heat the oil in a nonstick pan, add the patties and quickly fry for 3 min on each side.

Serve with tomato salsa, green salad and toasted pittas.

Nutritional value per serving: 274kcal, 42g carbs (7g fiber, 4g sugar), 1 g fat, 8g protein, 12% iron, 12% magnesium, 18% vitamin A, 31% vitamin C, 28% vitamin B6, 20% vitamin B9.

29. Cucumber and Cranberry Salad

Enjoy a simple bed of greens with juicy cherry tomatoes, sweet dried cranberries and ripe olives that add color, flavor and a welcomed amount of vitamins to your meal. Make your own spice mix and store in an airtight container for up to 6 months.

Ingredients (2 servings):

3 cups mixed salad greens

1 cup fresh spinach

1 cup cherry tomatoes, halved

1 medium cucumber, chopped

2 tablespoon olive oil

2 tablespoons lemon juice

2 tablespoons water

1 ¼ teaspoons homemade spice mix

Homemade spice mix:

½ teaspoon ground cumin

½ teaspoon ground coriander

½ teaspoon paprika

¼ teaspoon ground turmeric

¼ teaspoon garlic powder

1/8 teaspoon cayenne pepper

Prep time: 20 min

No cooking

Preparation:

In a large bowl, combine the salad greens, spinach, tomatoes, cucumber, cranberries and olives.

In a small crew-top jar, mix the olive oil, water, seasoning and lemon juice and shake well.

Pour the dressing over the vegetable mixture, toss to coat, divide between 2 bowls and serve.

Nutritional value per serving: 212kcal, 19g carbs (3g fiber, 10g sugar), 16g fat (2g saturated), 2g protein, 11% iron, 31% vitamin A, 35% vitamin C, 12% vitamin E, 132% vitamin K, 10% vitamin B9.

30. Quinoa Pilaf

Try a low-calorie vegetarian dinner that boasts a high amount of vitamin A. Quinoa and butternut squash work well together, while the crunchy almonds add some healthy fats to your meal.

Ingredients (2 servings):

2 cups butternut squash, peeled and cubed

1 cup cooked quinoa

3 cloves garlic, minced

1/8 cup almond, sliced

1 tablespoon olive oil

1/8 teaspoon red pepper, crushed

1 teaspoon fresh sage, snipped

¼ teaspoon salt

Prep time: 10 min

Cooking time: 30 min

Preparation:

Preheat the oven to 220C fan/ gas 7. Combine the butternut squash, garlic and red pepper and half of the olive oil in a large bowl. Stir until the squash is evenly coated the spoon into a baking pan and roast for 30 min. Stir once and add the almonds for the last 5 min.

In a large bowl, combine the quinoa, remaining olive oil, sage and salt, then add in the squash and almonds. Stir all the ingredients together then serve.

Nutritional value per serving: 287kcal, 43g carbs (3g fiber, 4g sugar), 12g fat (1g saturated), 7g protein, 10% calcium, 15% iron, 34% magnesium, 457% vitamin A, 52g vitamin C, 29% vitamin E, 17% vitamin B1, 11% vitamin B2, 13% vitamin B3, 18% vitamin B6, 20% vitamin B9.

31. Avocado and Grapefruit Salad

A low-carb, vitamin-packed meal, the avocado and grapefruit salad is a perfect blend of citrusy taste and creamy texture. Delicious and high in healthy fats, the avocado is great way to add flavor to any salad.

Ingredients (2 servings):

4 cups fresh baby spinach

1 grapefruit, sectioned

½ avocado, sliced

1 tablespoon olive oil

1 tablespoon raspberry vinegar

1 teaspoon water

½ teaspoon brown sugar

a pinch of salt

Prep time: 5 min

No cooking

Preparation:

Arrange the spinach, grapefruit and avocado slices on a serving platter.

Whisk together the raspberry vinegar, olive oil, water, sugar and salt in a small bowl.

Drizzle the dressing over the spinach mixture and serve.

Nutritional value per serving: 209kcal, 19g carbs (5g fiber, 8g sugar), 14g fat (2g saturated), 4g protein, 12% iron, 18% magnesium, 141% vitamin A, 102% vitamin C, 111% vitamin E, 380% vitamin K, 10% vitamin A, 11% vitamin B2, 10% vitamin B5, 15% vitamin B6, 44% vitamin B9.

32. Chickpea Soup

Add a sprinkle of fresh parsley leaves to this zesty soup that packs Moroccan flavors and veggie-based, healthy carbs. This low-calorie soup is a great option for an end of the day meal.

Ingredients (2 servings):

200g can chickpeas, rinsed and drained

200g canned tomatoes, chopped

1 clove garlic, minced

½ medium onion, chopped

1 medium celery stick, chopped

50g frozen broad beans

300ml hot vegetable stock

1 teaspoon ground cumin

Juice and zest for ¼ lemon

a pinch of ground black pepper

a pinch of salt

Prep time: 20 min

Cooking time: 25 min

Preparation:

Heat the oil in a saucepan then fry the celery, onion and garlic for 10 min, stirring frequently. Tip in the cumin and fry for another min.

Turn the heat up, add the stock, tomatoes, chickpeas and black pepper and simmer for 8 min. Throw in the broad beans and lemon juice and cook for another 2 min. Add the salt, then top with the lemon zest and serve.

Nutritional value per serving: 181kcal, 36g carbs (6g fiber, 5g sugar), 1g fat, 8g protein, 16% iron, 13% magnesium, 25% vitamin C, 10% vitamin K, 28% vitamin B6, 27% vitamin B9.

33. Grilled Vegetable Salad

Try a high-fiber, vitamin-packed light supper that blends different types of veggies and makes perfect use of your grill. Serve with some torn mozzarella for a more tangy taste.

Ingredients (2 servings):

1 eggplant, cut into 1 cm rounds

2 onions, sliced ½ cm thick but kept as whole slices

6 sundried tomatoes in oil, drained and cut into strips

6 black olives

2 red bell peppers

1 garlic clove, crushed

1 red chili, finely chopped

2 tablespoons olive oil

1 tablespoon wine vinegar

a handful basil, roughly torn

Prep time: 20 min

Cooking time: 1 h

Preparation:

Blacken the peppers under a hot grill then put them in a bowl, cover and leave to cool.

Mix the oil, vinegar, garlic and chili in a bowl. On a hot griddle pan, grill the eggplant and onion in batches until they have grill marks on both sides and start to soften. When the vegetables are ready, put them into the dressing to marinate, breaking the onions up into rings.

When the peppers are cool enough to handle, peel and remove the stalk and seeds. Cut into strips and toss into the bowl where the rest of the vegetables have been left to marinate. Mix in the tomatoes, olives, and basil, season to taste and serve.

Nutritional value per serving: 285kcal, 33g carbs (12g fiber, 15g sugar), 14g fat (2g saturated), 4g protein, 18% magnesium, 79% vitamin A, 290% vitamin C, 22% vitamin E, 28% vitamin K, 13% vitamin B1, 16% vitamin B2, 17% vitamin B3, 11% vitamin B5, 33% vitamin B6, 31% vitamin B9.

34. Tofu Dinner

A vegan friendly meal with a good amount of minerals and protein, this tofu dinner excels in blending sweet and spicy flavors. Serve with a side of steamed cauliflower to add more vitamins to the mix.

Ingredients (4 servings):

800g tofu

½ cup soy sauce

2 tablespoons sesame oil

1 tablespoon olive oil

1 tablespoon chili flakes

4 garlic cloves, minced

1 tablespoon ginger, freshly grated

salt, to taste

Prep time: 5 min

Cooking time: 15 min

Preparation:

Mix the soy sauce, sesame oil, ginger, chili flakes and salt in a bowl and set aside.

Pour olive oil into a sauce pan and heat then fry the tofu for about 10 min.

Pour the sauce into the pan and cook for 3-5 min. Serve when the sauce has thickened and the tofu is done.

Nutritional value per serving: 185kcal, 4g carbs (2g fiber, 2g sugar), 15g fat (3g saturated), 18g protein, 34% calcium, 19% iron, 19% magnesium, 11% vitamin B2, 11% vitamin B6.

35. Pea and Artichoke Purée

Try a fresh meal that takes only 15 min to make and is low in calories and carbs. Served chilled, it makes a wonderful addition to a summer diet and it livens up your table with a nice splash of green.

Ingredients (2 servings):

100g artichoke heart, from a jar

140g frozen small peas

1 tablespoon ground cumin

2 tablespoon lemon juice

2 tablespoons olive oil

a small handful of mint leaves

a pinch of salt

a pinch of pepper

Prep time: 10 min

Cooking time: 5 min

Preparation:

Tip the peas into a bowl and cover with boiling water. Leave for 5 min, then drain and tip into a food processor with the rest of the ingredients and seasoning. Pulse until you make a rough purée, then spoon into a bowl and cover with cling film. Serve when it has chilled.

Nutritional value per serving: 198kcal, 15g carbs (7g fiber, 3g sugar), 14g fat (2g saturated), 4g protein, 12% magnesium, 30% vitamin A, 22% vitamin C, 34% vitamin K, 15% vitamin B1, 18% vitamin B9.

SNACKS

1. Apple and Peanut Butter

Slice 1 small apple and spread 1 tablespoon creamy peanut butter on the pieces.

Nutritional value: 189kcal, 4g protein, 28g carbs (5g fiber, 20g sugar), 8g fat (1g saturated), 14% vitamin C, 14% vitamin B3.

2. Greek Yogurt with Strawberries.

Mix 150g Greek Yogurt with 5 medium-sized strawberries cut in half.

Nutritional value: 150kcal, 11g protein, 10g carbs (10g sugar), 8g fat (5g saturated), 10% calcium, 60% vitamin C.

3. Cup of Popcorn

Nutritional value: 31kcal, 1g protein, 6g carbs (1g fiber).

4. Smoothie

In a blender, mix ½ cup blueberries, 1 cup spinach leaves, ½ cup low-fat Greek Yogurt and ½ cup pineapple coconut water.

Nutritional value: 168kcal, 24g carbs (3g fiber, 8g sugar), 17g protein, 23% calcium, 57% vitamin A, 73% vitamin C, 199% vitamin K, 16% vitamin 9.

5. Trail Mix

Combine ½ cup whole grain cereal, 2 tablespoons of raisins and 12 almonds.

Nutritional value per serving: 222kcal, 35g carbs (4g fiber, 15g sugar), 9g fat, 2g protein, 10% magnesium, 18% vitamin E.

6. Cucumber and Ranch Dressing

Slice 1 cup of cucumber and top with 1 tablespoon of ranch dressing.

Nutritional value: 89kcal, 5g carbs (2g sugar), 8g fat (1g saturated), 45% vitamin K.

7. Ham and Pineapple

Cut 30g of thinly sliced turkey ham into long strips and fold the slices like an accordion. Skewer the folded ham slices with chuck of pineapple (3/4 cup).

Nutritional value: 100kcal, 15g carbs (2g fiber, 13g sugar), 2g fat, 5g protein, 95% vitamin C.

8. Fresh Fruit Parfait

Layer up ¼ cup granola with ¼ cup blueberries, ¼ cup raspberries and ¼ cup fat-free cottage cheese.

Nutritional value: 204kcal, 29g carbs (2g fiber, 12g sugar), 3g fat, 9g protein, 44% vitamin C, 10% vitamin K.

9. Rye Crisps

Spread 2 rye crisps with 2 tablespoon light cream cheese and top with ¼ cup sliced cucumber.

Nutritional value: 138kcal, 35g carbs (6g fiber, 2g sugar), 8g fat (2g saturated), 4g protein.

10. Veggie Dip

Dip fresh cut veggies (1 cup of green peppers/broccoli/celery/cauliflower) into 1/3 cup hummus.

Nutritional value: 141kcal, 12g carbs (5g fiber), 8g fat (1g saturated), 6g protein, 11% vitamin A, 15% magnesium, 11% vitamin C, 78% vitamin K, 10% vitamin B10, 17% vitamin B9.

11. Carrots with Ranch Dressing

Dip 10 baby carrots in 2 tablespoons ranch dressing.

Nutritional value: 181kcal, 10g carbs (3g fiber, 6 g sugar), 16g fat (2g saturated), 1g protein, 276% vitamin A, 58% vitamin K.

12. Pear and Cheese

Slice a small pear and serve it with a light cheese stick.

Nutritional value: 146kcal, 26g carbs (5g fiber, 15g sugar), 3g fat (2g saturated), 7g protein, 10% vitamin C.

13. Roasted Soy Beans

Nutritional value for 20g: 155kcal, 11g carbs (2g fiber), 7g fat (1g saturated), 11g protein.

14. Cherry Tomatoes with Cottage Cheese

Cut 5 cherry tomatoes in half and smear them with 2 tablespoons cottage cheese mixed with fresh dill and a pinch of salt.

Nutritional value: 58kcal, 4g protein, 10g carbs, 30% vitamin A, 40% vitamin C, 20% vitamin K, 10% vitamin B1, 10% vitamin B6, 10% vitamin B9.

OTHER GREAT TITLES BY THIS AUTHOR

Advanced Mental Toughness Training for Bodybuilders

Using Visualization to Push Yourself to the Limit

By

Joseph Correa

Certified Sports Nutritionist

Becoming Mentally Tougher in Bodybuilding by Using Meditation

Reach Your Potential by Controlling Your Inner Thoughts

By

Joseph Correa

Certified Sports Nutritionist

www.ingramcontent.com/pod-product-compliance
Lightning Source LLC
Chambersburg PA
CBHW071744080526
44588CB00013B/2145